A. B. Rich

Gleanings from the Fields of Science, Art and History

Or, Incidental Testimony to the Inspiration of the Scriptures

A. B. Rich

Gleanings from the Fields of Science, Art and History
Or, Incidental Testimony to the Inspiration of the Scriptures

ISBN/EAN: 9783337184131

Printed in Europe, USA, Canada, Australia, Japan

Cover: Foto ©ninafisch / pixelio.de

More available books at **www.hansebooks.com**

GLEANINGS

FROM THE FIELDS OF

SCIENCE, ART AND HISTORY:

OR,

INCIDENTAL TESTIMONY

TO THE

INSPIRATION OF THE SCRIPTURES.

BY REV. A. B. RICH, BEVERLY, MASS.

WRITTEN FOR THE MASSACHUSETTS SABBATH SCHOOL SOCIETY, AND APPROVED BY THE COMMITTEE OF PUBLICATION.

BOSTON:
MASSACHUSETTS SABBATH SCHOOL SOCIETY,
DEPOSITORY, NO. 13 CORNHILL.

Entered, according to Act of Congress, in the year 1864,
BY THE MASSACHUSETTS SABBATH SCHOOL SOCIETY,
In the Clerk's Office of the District Court of Massachusetts.

Electrotyped and Printed by Wright & Potter, No. 4 Spring Lane.

CONTENTS.

	PAGE.

CHAPTER I.
The Rosetta Stone.—The Zodiac of Dendera. . 9

CHAPTER II.
Physical Features of Egypt. 24

CHAPTER III.
Shishak.—King of Egypt.—Relics and Sculptures. 27

CHAPTER IV.
The Flood.—Noah's Ark. 33

CHAPTER V.
Tower of Babel.—Confusion of Tongues. . . 36

CHAPTER VI.
Babylon.—Nebuchadnezzar's Insanity. . . 41

CHAPTER VII.
Overthrow of Babylon.—Belshazzar's Feast.—A Discrepancy Reconciled.—Daniel's Promotion. 45

CHAPTER VIII.
Nineveh.—Sculptures.—Prophecy of Nahum. . 49

CHAPTER IX.
Sennacherib.—His Invasion of Judea.—Jerusalem.—Lachish.—His Death. 52

CONTENTS.

CHAPTER X.
Prophecy of Jonah.—Jonah's Gourd. . . . 60

CHAPTER XI.
Ezekiel's Vision.—Tammuz. 64

CHAPTER XII.
Cavern of Bezetha.—Solomon's Temple. . . 69

CHAPTER XIII.
Early Spread of Christianity.—Persecutions.—Catacombs of Rome.—Sculptures. . . . 74

CHAPTER XIV.
Paul at Athens.—At Ephesus.—The Goddess Diana.—Asiarchs.—Town Clerk. . . . 82

CHAPTER XV.
Roman Government as seen in "Luke," and "The Acts of the Apostles." 87

CHAPTER XVI.
"The Foolish Galatians."—The French. . . 90

CHAPTER XVII.
Science.—Circulation of the Blood.—Weight of the Atmosphere.—The Pleiades.—The Firmament. 95

CHAPTER XVIII.
Manners and Customs of Bible Lands. . . 104

CHAPTER XIX.
Conclusion. 107

PREFACE.

READER, have you ever been present in a court of justice, where witnesses are examined, and lawyers plead? If so, you will understand the value of *incidental* evidence, that which comes out casually, as men say, and without premeditation. You will remember how different individuals, strangers to each other, and without concert, and while each was laboring to serve his own ends, *seemed* nevertheless, on that occasion, to have been conspiring together for years perhaps, to screen the innocent from suspicion, or to hedge up the path of the transgressor, and bring his crime to the light of day. You will remember too, how numerous providences seemed to have been so arranged as to secure beyond a peradventure the same results. At the right moment, and under the best circumstances for the detection of crime, or the proof of innocence, "That which was spoken in darkness was heard in the light, and that which was spoken in the ear in closets, was proclaimed upon the house-tops."

In the progress of worldly events, facts have occurred, histories have been written, notes of travel and discovery have been made, the monuments of past ages have been exhumed; all of which stand in relation more or less intimate with the historic data of the Book of God. They all have a testimony, which they are able to give, if interrogated, for the Inspiration of the Christian Scriptures.

In an age when German Rationalism, French Pantheism, and English Criticism are all conspiring to undermine our confidence in these Divine Revelations, the author of this little work has thought it might be well to glean some of the scattered ears from the fields of Science, Art, and History, and bind them into a sheaf, as an offering on the sacred altar of Truth. He makes no pretense to a full discussion of the subject in hand, —the incidental evidence that the Scriptures are inspired; that those who wrote them were Divinely secured against error, and received revelations from God. His aim has simply been, by selecting salient facts, here and there, to suggest thought and study, and to incite the reader to note for himself the evidence that lies all around him, that the writings we call " the Scriptures," are indeed "given by *inspiration of God*, and are profitable for doctrine, for reproof, for correction, for instruction in righteousness; that the man of God may be perfect, thoroughly furnished unto all good works."

"The Bible! that's the Book. The Book indeed!
    The Book of books:
    On which who looks,
As he should do aright, shall never need

Wish for a better light
To guide him in the right.

"It is the Book of God. What if I should
Say, god of books?
Let him that looks
Angry at the expression, as too bold,
His thoughts in silence smother,
Till he can find such another."

BEVERLY, MASS., July 15, 1863.

GLEANINGS.

CHAPTER 1.

The Rosetta Stone.—The Zodiac of Dendera.

DURING the years 1798 and 1799, the Emperor Napoleon I., and the literary men attached to his expedition into Egypt, might have been often seen gathered together to discuss scientific questions, and examine the numerous relics, which, in that land of antiquity, were every day brought to their notice. Not the Pyramids, the Sphinx, the city of the dead, Luxor and Karnak, alone attracted their attention. Objects less conspicuous and striking—the smaller temples, the deities sculptured upon their walls, and the numerous inscriptions that covered their sacred buildings, their monuments, and their utensils, (all in a then unknown language,)—these also were suggestive of topics for individual and concerted study.

At first the ignorant Arabs regarded those enthusiastic *savans* as priests; afterwards as alchymists; not being able to comprehend their interest in those old ruins, sculptures, and inscriptions. They at length concluded that the French had some traditionary evidence that those enduring monuments were built by their remote ancestors. It mattered little to those antiquarians what was thought of their labors. Their mission was research and discovery, not the enlightenment of the Bedouin Arabs.

Two minor objects especially attracted their notice—the "*Rosetta Stone*," and the "*Zodiac of Dendera.*" When the troops were building the fort St. Julien, at Rosetta, they came upon a mutilated block of basalt, containing an inscription in three characters —the *Hieratic*, or sacred text of the old Egyptians; the Demotic, or popular language; and the Greek. This inscription proved to be a decree of the Egyptian priests in honor of Ptolemy Epiphanes. It contained these words, "This decree shall be engraved on hard stone, in sacred, common, and Greek characters," (ἱεροις και ἐγχωριοις και ἑλληνικοις γραμμασιν.) Subsequently this stone fell into the hands of the English, and was deposited in the British Museum. By a comparison of the two former inscriptions in unknown texts with the Greek, the key was at length discovered to the common and sacred characters of the ancient Egyptians, and, by means of these, to the more ancient system of hieroglyphics. Thus, by this "master-piece of criticism," as it has been justly called, the monuments and relics of that "Cradle of Science," ancient Egypt, have been made intelligible.

When the French entered Dendera, a small village in the vicinity of Thebes, they were surprised beyond measure at the extent and magnificence of its ruins. They came upon the remains of a vast temple, every feature of which, "from the colossal figures of Isis, which support the entablature of the vestibule, to the smallest hieroglyphics, seemed to have come from fairy land. So universal was this impression, that the meanest soldiers of the army paused to examine those sacred relics, and declared with one voice, that this sight alone was enough to indemnify for the fatigue of the whole campaign."

The vestibules, halls, and chambers of this Temple of Isis were covered with hieroglyphics. Those upon the ceiling of the portico were *astronomical* figures and emblems, conspicuous among which were the *twelve signs of the zodiac*. On the ceiling of a small apartment in the upper story, the same representation was repeated. Of all these sculptures the French made the most accurate drawings possible, and carried them to Paris. The attention of learned Europeans was at once enlisted, and they set themselves in earnest to the task of deciphering them. The representation of the twelve signs of the zodiac copied from the ceiling of the little chapel especially attracted their notice, from its apparent relation to the *precession of the equinoxes.*

As the earth moves round the sun once in a year, the sun *appears* to make a great circle among the stars. But if its position be carefully observed at the vernal equinox, it will be found, that when it comes to the equator the following spring, it does not occupy *precisely* the same position as it did the year before. The equinox happens sooner than we should have expected. The equinoctial point seems to have *moved backwards*, (or in a direction opposite to the earth's motion,) *about* 50″ of a degree. In the course of 72 years its apparent motion equals an entire degree. In other words, at the vernal equinox the sun appears to be one degree westward of its position 72 years before. But one degree is the $\frac{1}{360}$ part of the whole circle of the heavens. Hence, in about 25,920 years, (72×360,) accurately,

25,868, the sun will seem to have made *the entire circuit of the heavens.*

The moment the *savans* of Europe saw those drawings of the zodiac, they supposed they had before them the evidence of the very great antiquity of the temple from which they were taken. They saw that the signs had been divided by a line drawn between Cancer and Leo, and that the sun and moon had been represented at this point. And *assuming* that the builders of the temple had the same knowledge of the sun's apparent motion in the zodiac that we have, and that they designed to represent its position when the temple was built, they supposed they were able to determine *the number of years since it was built.* And so they would have been, had their assumptions been correct. Unfortunately for their theories they were both false.

But what, according to their reckoning, was the result? If they regarded the sun and moon as indicating the position of the *winter solstice* at that time, the vernal equinox would have been in Libra, or nearly eight entire signs from its present position. This supposition would give about 17,000 years for the age of the temple. ($8 \times 30 \times 72$.)

If they assumed that the sun and moon indicated the position of the *vernal equinox*, this would remove it nearly five signs from its present position, requiring for its recession about 10,000 years. ($5 \times 30 \times 72$.)

Some there were, indeed, who reasoned upon the supposition, equally natural, that the sun and moon were represented as in the *summer solstice*, which would bring the vernal equinox in Taurus, or only about 45 degrees from its present position. This change would be effected in about 3,000 years. (45×72.) This supposition would fix the date of the temple about 12,000 years B. C.

But this small number did not satisfy infidelity. It fixed upon the higher as undoubtedly the truth, and rung the changes upon them for about thirty years.

If that temple had been built 17,000, or only 10,000 years, what could follow, but that the Bible was a cheat, and the Mosaic account of creation, which declared that that event took place less than 6,000 years ago, was a lie. It was demonstrated! It was mathematically certain! Infidelity was wild with excitement. It was trumpeted over the continent as the great discovery of the 19th century—the Bible a cheat, a hoax, and Christians a company of dupes. From the hand of one of the professors of the

University of Breslau went forth a pamphlet entitled, "Invincible Proof that our Earth is at least ten times older than taught by the Bible." More than fifty publications of a similar import were issued, while the thought was echoed and re-echoed in newspapers and periodicals all over Europe. The supposed "invincible proof" was paraded before all eyes, and it was thrust into the teeth of all Christians, that the bubble of Christianity had burst, and was henceforth to be regarded as obsolete.

Christians had little to say in defence. They could not disprove the argument for want of data. They could only wait, suffer, and pray for light. But they knew they had not "followed cunningly devised fables."

So great was the desire of the French to possess the original sculpture, that in 1820

Lelorraine set sail for Egypt to obtain it. Mohammed Ali permitted its removal. The Arab huts that had been built upon the top of the ruins were removed, together with the rubbish that had been accumulating for ages. By means of chisels, saws, and gunpowder, that part of the ceiling which contained the zodiac circle was cut out, slid down to the banks of the Nile, and transported to Paris, yet blackened with the smoke and soot of the sacrificial fires which ages agone the old Egyptians had kindled there, in their idolatrous rites. It was deposited in the National Library, and was indeed a notable relic, even if not seventeen thousand years old. So great was the crowd that flocked to see it, that the king was compelled to "deposit it in a dark chamber, while the multitude cursed both kings and priests for combining, as they said, to keep the people from becoming enlightened."

Meanwhile, by the labors of Dr. Young, Dr. Lacy, Champollion, and others, the Egyptian hieroglyphics had been deciphered. The way was now prepared to study the *sciences* of the Egyptians. And it was discovered, (alas, how short is the triumphing of the wicked!) that the assumptions upon which their argument had been based had no foundation in truth. That the location of the sun and moon between Cancer and Leo had no connection whatever with the precession of the equinoxes, with the sun's place among the constellations, or its apparent motion along the zodiac. That it simply indicated their joint rule over the constellations, "one-half being assigned to the sun, and the other half to the moon." Their theories, based upon ignorance, exploded like a bubble. Their great eagerness to oust Christianity and the Christian's Bible, had led them to commit a most silly blunder, and to bring upon themselves the derision of the whole world.

But this was not the end of the drama. Haman is to be hung upon his own gallows. That mute sandstone was able to testify concerning its age, the age of the temple it had adorned, and the emperor who built it. Now that its sculptures were understood, they were seen to indicate the date of the birth of the builder of the temple, and to point unmistakably to A. D. 37. But this date answered to the birth of Nero. On the edge of the slab was found part of an oval, or cartouch, with some of the letters of a name. The remainder was left at Dendera, the saw having divided it when the slab was taken from the ceiling. By sending to

Egypt for a drawing of the remainder, it was found to contain the hieroglyphics of the name of the 6th Cæsar—Nero. These results were all confirmed by a comparison with the drawings they had made of the sculptures upon other portions of the temple.

Here was proof that could not be gainsayed. Infidelity blushed as it read on that sooty relic, A. D. 37, not B. C. 17,000, and since 1832, has shown little disposition to revert to the Zodiac of Dendera.

These antiquarian researches constitute *an epoch* in the history of scientific and ethnographic study. They illustrate the tendency that has prevailed in every age to turn every scientific discovery against the Christian religion and the Book of God. And they show the *nature of the evidence*, that is continually coming to the light, in support of the inspiration of the Christian Scriptures.

Indirect, incidental evidence is regarded as scarcely inferior to that which is positive, in any court of justice. It is rapidly accumulating in our day. Let us gather up and place side by side several isolated facts, enough to see the nature and strength of this kind of evidence for the truth of the Christian Scriptures.

Let us begin with Egypt, where we are brought by the consideration of the foregoing discoveries.

CHAPTER II.

Physical Features of Egypt.

WHEN Moses had grown to manhood, his indignation was roused by the oppressions to which the Jewish captives were subjected. Seeing an Egyptian smiting a Hebrew, he took the part of the oppressed and killed the Egyptian, "and hid him in the sand." (Ex. 2 : 12.) To this latter fact, casually introduced, we may refer, to test the truth of the narrative. "*He hid him in the sand,*" evidently in a hastily dug grave.

Look now at the soil along the Nile; not heavy or clayey, like that washed by the Euphrates. Then the allusion would have

cast doubt upon the veracity of the narrative. Dr. Robinson, after speaking of the exhilaration of a voyage up the Nile, adds—
"Yet if the traveler set foot on shore, the romance of his river voyage will quickly be dissipated. He will find the soil becoming an almost impalpable powder under his feet, *through which he must wade to the next village.*"

In such a soil how easy the burial of a human body; how natural this method of disposing of it, when the next gust of wind from the desert would smooth the surface and obliterate all traces of the deed!

How exactly conformed to the geography of the country is another incident in the story of Egyptian bondage. To prevent the increase of the Hebrews, Pharaoh issued this order: "Every son that is born to the Hebrews, ye shall cast into the river."

(Ex. 1: 22.) The river Nile was the most important feature of Egypt. Throwing the infants into it would be the most ready method of their destruction. But such an order would have been irrelevant in Palestine, or in numerous countries on the globe. And travelers have demonstrated that the land of Goshen, where the Hebrews lived, was on the eastern, or Pelusiac branch of the Nile. There is a *naturalness* and *adaptation* in the record of the physical features of Egypt that confirms its truth.

CHAPTER III.

Shishak.—King of Egypt.—Relics and Sculptures.

IN 1 Kings, 14: 25, 26, and 2 Chron. 12: 2—4, we have an account of the invasion of Judea by Shishak, King of Egypt. "Twelve hundred chariots, and three score thousand horsemen, and footmen without number;" such was his army. "And he took the fenced (walled) cities which pertained to Judah, the treasures of the Lord's house, and of the king's house, and made Rehoboam and his people his servants." He returned to Egypt and made a record of that invasion in sculpture, upon the walls of the great temple of Karnac.

"A colossal figure," says Robinson, "is seen advancing in his chariot, holding in his hand ten cords, which are attached to as many rows of captives that follow behind him." This was evidently a representation of his triumphal entry into Thebes, on his return. Amidst these figures, and filling up the history of the campaign, are the names, "Kingdom of Judah," "Megiddo," "Hebron," "Beth-shan," "Taanak," "Valley of Hinnom," and the "Great Place," or Jerusalem.

The Rosetta Stone was not discovered in vain. Who shall say that *its discovery* was not the great purpose in the mind of God, of Napoleon's expedition into Egypt? "Nevertheless, he meant it not so, neither did his heart think so."

In Dr. Abbott's Museum of Egyptian Antiquities, in the city of New York, there may be seen the *breast-plate* of this same Shishak, made of iron scales, perhaps worn in this very expedition, a relic more than twenty-seven hundred years old, brought to light in this age to confirm these ancient Hebrew records.

In that collection, there is a vase of green earthen-ware, "found in the plain of Zoar," bearing the name of Zerah, the Egyptian king, who made war upon king Asa with more than a million of men, but was signally defeated. (2 Chron. 14: 9—15.) We should not expect to find any *monumental* records of this invasion, since it was unsuccessful and disastrous. This small relic, however, testified to the *existence of such a character*, and thus aids in giving validity to the record in the Chronicles.

There, too, are seen numerous specimens of brick, from the ruins of Thebes, Sakharah, and Heliopolis, some of which bear the stamp of Thothmes III., the Pharaoh who "made the lives of the Israelites bitter with hard bondage in mortar and in brick." (Ex. 1: 14.) Those very brick may have been moulded by their hands. The straw that is seen in them, as they crumble to pieces, may have been gathered by them from the fields to add to their already too heavy burdens.

A recent American traveler has testified, that "In the tomb of Roschere—the overseer of public buildings under Thothmes III.—we saw the whole process of brick-making depicted. Some are digging and mixing the clay; others shaping it in the mould; others are taking the bricks from the form; and others carrying them away to be dried. In another tomb the mode of reaping grain is illustrated. It is cut a little below the ear, and the straw left standing in the field. In fact, we saw almost the entire history of Joseph and the Israelites pictured upon the tombs, and sculptured upon the monuments of ancient Egypt."

Not only have the monumental records of that ancient land been deciphered, but the papyri, or books, some of which are still preserved. And there are found the names of Moses, and James, who, Paul says, "withstood him." Moses is represented as a worker of miracles; as the leader of a people who marched eastward, by the route of Mizdol and Zoar; who had a contest with the Egyptians at a place of a great waterflood; and a reference is made to the mysterious death of one of the royal youth, perhaps the one Moses slew and hid in the sand.

These are some of the relics which have

already been gleaned from the land of the Pharaohs, to illustrate the truth of the Pentateuch. So far as any references have been found to places, persons, or events described by Moses, they confirm his narrative.

CHAPTER IV.

The Flood.—Noah's Ark.

One of the earliest historic events narrated by Moses is the account of the flood. Is his narrative confirmed by any data in our possession? Yes, the *dimensions of the ark*, as there given, testify to its inspiration. He affirms that God gave to Noah those dimensions.

What now, according to the light which naval architecture has shed upon the subject, was the nature of that model? If uncouth and disproportioned, it did not originate with God, who knows all the laws of wind and water, the strength of materials, and the equilibrium of floating bodies. Modern architects acknowledge that the proportions given are found to be the very ones best adapted to the construction of a vessel in order that it may receive and transport in safety the greatest possible tunnage.

Let us consider this fact, connected with the first water-craft of which we have any knowledge. It was an immense structure, equivalent to almost a score of first-rate men-of-war. Its model was perfect. And yet Moses was not a ship-builder; not a seaman; had never in his life crossed but one sea, and that "on dry land." How could he have known the perfect proportions for modeling a vessel, which have taxed the powers of nautical science and human ingenuity for centuries? It is manifestly impossible! And the same impossibility will present itself whosoever we may assume to have originated the model in that early age. It *must have come from God*, as Moses affirms. This narrative, then, stands as a witness to the truth of his account of the flood. This account being true, the early wickedness of the race follows, and the credibility of all Moses wrote.

CHAPTER V.

Tower of Babel.—Confusion of Tongues.

THE foundations of Babylon were laid soon after the flood, in the mad project of men to scale heaven by a tower, and make themselves a name in the earth. Moses represents the builders as counseling together in this language: "Let us make brick, and burn them thoroughly." (Gen. 11: 3.)

Now a traveler, roaming over Assyria with this statement in his hand, would feel that the *physical features of the country* might be referred to, to confirm or invalidate its claim to inspiration. And what would he find? A rocky region, supplying to their hand the materials for an enduring structure, such as the Tower of Babel was designed to be? Then what need of brick? Or a sandy soil, deprived of the necessary ingredients for their manufacture? Then what possibility?

The facts, as stated by modern travelers, are simply these. Stone quarries are, and ever have been, utterly unknown throughout the whole region of Babylon, while the soil is remarkably fitted for the manufacture of brick. It consists of a fine clay mixed with sand. With this, as the waters of the river retire, its banks are covered. This compost furnished the finest materials existing for brick-making. And so "thoroughly did they burn them," that the tooth of time has not yet been able to devour them. They come forth from their mounds of rubbish as sound as when laid by those ancient masons, and covered with inscriptions in the old

Assyrian character. They have a resurrection in this sceptical age to testify to the inspiration of Moses, and the truth of his narrative, though writing of events that transpired long before his day, and of a land he had never visited.

Again, Moses tells us *in what* those bricks were laid. "Slime," or bitumen, "had they for mortar." (Gen. 11: 3.) And the traveler finds along the banks of the Euphrates, and near the site of the city, this natural cement, boiling up like water from the earth. Layard discovered the same phenomenon in the vicinity of ancient Nineveh, and illustrates the reference here made to the use of this bitumen instead of mortar. Speaking of the removal of some colossal lions from the palace of Nimroud, he says: "The sculptures rested simply upon the platform of sun-dried bricks, without any other substructure, *a mere layer of bitumen, about an inch thick*, having been placed under the plinth." (*Nineveh and Babylon*, vol. ii., p. 203.)

Here, then, is circumstantial evidence, confirming the narrative of Moses in several particulars. They made brick because the country afforded no supply of stone. They used bitumen for cement because they had no lime for mortar. The bricks themselves show that they were "burned thoroughly," and not merely sun-dried. The inscriptions show their date. These coincidences show that the story of Babel is not a mere human record, a happy guess, a fabrication, or a myth. It is God's record of human folly, "written for our learning."

There is another striking incident connected with this transaction. "The Lord did then confound the language of all the earth, and they left off to build the city." (Gen. 11: 7—9.) One proof of this is the diversity of tongues actually existing among the different races and tribes of mankind. Another is found in the traditions respecting the origin of this diversity, as preserved by Berosus, Abydenus, and Polyhistor, all of which are strikingly conformed to the statements of Moses. They all agree in respect to the *three prominent features* of Moses' narrative. The race was *previously of one speech;* the confusion occurred *in connection with the Tower of Babel;* and the *work of building was stayed* in consequence.

CHAPTER VI.

Babylon.—Nebuchadnezzar's Insanity.

BABEL became the nucleus of Babylon, and gave the city and province its name. Around it men gathered, built their habitations, and dwelt by millions as the centuries rolled on. Nebuchadnezzar greatly enlarged and beautified it, and, proud of the magnificence he had given to the city, exclaimed, while surveying it from the roof of his palace—

"Is not this great Babylon that I have built for the house of my kingdom, by the might of my power, and for the honor of my majesty?" (Dan. 4: 29, 30.)

Recently, by the enterprise of Layard and others, the ruins of that city have been laid open to the light. "They consist principally," says Layard, "of loose bricks, tiles, and fragments of stone. The bricks are of a pale yellow color, and upon nearly every one are clearly and deeply stamped the name and titles of Nebuchadnezzar." More than twenty-three hundred years have passed since that boastful speech was made on the roof of his palace; and now its ruins come forth to illustrate the record of the Jewish prophet whom he had carried away captive in the sack of Jerusalem.

Daniel records the circumstances that attended his speech—the fearful malady, or temporary insanity that came upon him, when "he was driven from men, and made his dwelling with the beasts, and did eat grass as oxen." (Dan. 4: 33.) He recovered; and it was doubtless with reference to this affliction that he caused an inscription to be made of which Rawlinson has given us the following translation :—

"Four years (?) . . . the seat of my kingdom in the city . . . which . . . did not rejoice my heart. In all my dominions I did not build a place of power; the precious treasures of my kingdom I did not lay up. In Babylon, buildings for myself and for the honor of my kingdom I did not lay out. In the worship of Merodach, my lord, the joy of my heart, (?) in Babylon, the city of his sovereignty and the seat of my empire, I did not sing his praises, (?) and I did not furnish his altars (with victims), nor did I clear out the canals." (Sir H. Rawlinson's Herodotus, vol. ii., pp. 585—587.)

It would not have been natural for a monarch to have allowed any very extended account of his insanity to descend to posterity. It is wonderful, shall we not say Providential, that he should cause so explicit a statement to be made, in the first person, as if on purpose to meet the cavils that might be raised against the credibility of Daniel, on the ground of the improbability of the transaction, and the want of other evidence? God provides for every exigency, and brings forward the evidence as fast as it is needed.

CHAPTER VII.

Overthrow of Babylon.—Belshazzar's Feast.—A Discrepancy Reconciled.—Daniel's Promotion.

DANIEL describes also the overthrow of Babylon by the Medo-Persian power. Its king, Belshazzar, was feasting in his palace. A hand as of a man is seen on the wall delineating his fate. "MENE, MENE, TEKEL, UPHARSIN." (Dan. 5 : 5, 25.) While these things are transpiring in the palace, Cyrus is marching his army through the bed of the Euphrates, and entering the city by the river gate. The palace is surrounded, and Belshazzar is slain. Such is the *sacred* history of the fall of Babylon and the death of her last king.

Berosus, however, the most reliable historian respecting that age and nation, asserts that the last king was Nabonadius, that he was not at Babylon when the city was taken, but had fled to Borsippa, where Cyrus subsequently found him, who, however did not slay him at all, but showed him great kindness.

Here is a discrepancy, from which Rationalists have argued the unhistorical character of Daniel's narrative, not only invalidating this statement, but bringing the truth of his whole book into doubt.

In 1854, Rawlinson discovered the records of the reign of Nabonadius, who was indeed the last king of the canon. And he finds that (as was not uncommon at that day) " Nabonadius had associated with him on the throne during the last years of his reign his son Bil-shar-uzur, (the Belshazzar of our translation,) and allowed him the royal title."

Here was a perfect reconciliation of the existing discrepancy. The two accounts were different, referring to different individuals, father and son. No doubt the account of Berosus is true respecting the taking of Nabonadius. No doubt the narrative of Daniel is true respecting the death of Belshazzar, at his feast, in his palace. The former event would most naturally attract the notice of the profane historian. The latter of the Hebrew prophet, who had been called in, in haste, to interpret the mysterious characters upon the wall.

This discovery, moreover, explains another allusion in the book of Daniel, which has heretofore been inexplicable. "If thou canst read the writing, and make known the interpretation thereof," said the king to Daniel respecting the mysterious words on the wall, " thou shalt be clothed in scarlet, and have a chain of gold about thy neck, and shalt be the *third ruler* in the kingdom." (Dan. 5 : 16.)

Why the *third* ruler, and not the second, as in the days of Nebuchadnezzar, who placed him next the throne ? (Dan. 2: 48.) The answer is easy. There were virtually *two kings* on the throne. Inferior to both father and son, he would be *the third* in rank. When the writing was interpreted, " Belshazzar commanded, and they clothed Daniel with scarlet, and put a chain of gold about his neck, and made a proclamation concerning him, that he should be the *third* ruler in the kingdom." (Dan. 5 : 29.)

CHAPTER VIII.

Nineveh.—Sculptures.—Prophecy of Nahum.

A FEW years since, through the kindness of Mr. Layard, and the influence of our missionaries at Mosul, there were sent to America, among other interesting relics, several large slabs of dark gypsum, taken from the ruins of ancient Nineveh. Upon each of them is sculptured, in bas-relief, a human figure; and across the drapery are inscriptions in the ancient cuneiform language.

Once those gypsum slabs lined the walls of the palace of Sennacherib. Once doubtless they received the idolatrous homage of the

Assyrians. Now they adorn the Museums of our Massachusetts Colleges, in the valley of the Connecticut, and among the hills of Berkshire. Dumb are they, though made in the likeness of men. And yet are they not eloquent witnesses to the truth of Moses and the prophets?

How rich in illustrations of the truth of the Scriptures are the ruins of ancient Nineveh—"*vetustissima sedes Assyriæ*," as Tacitus styles it.

The prophecy of Nahum is entitled "The burden of Nineveh. The book of the vision of Nahum the Elkoshite." (Nah. 1: 1.) The native place of this prophet—El-Kosh—still stands on the mountain side, some thirty miles north of Mosul. It was when looking down upon the Tigris valley, and the corrupt city, Nineveh, from his mountain home, that he wrote his prophecy. In the midst of his glowing description of its overthrow, he exclaims: "Take ye the spoil of silver, take the spoil of gold, for there is none end of the store and glory, out of all the pleasant furniture." And, as if looking on, until the pillage is completed, he adds: "She is empty, and void, and waste." (Nah. 2: 9, 10.)

Now the antiquarian in digging through and through those mounds of sculptures and hieroglyphics, finds nothing of gold or silver there. The spoil of these was all taken, though in the strong language of the prophet, as he saw that sack in vision, and the heaps of precious metals collected, "There was none end of them."

CHAPTER IX.

Sennacherib.—His Invasion of Judea.—Jerusalem.—Lachish.—His Death.

IN the Kings, the Chronicles, and Isaiah, we have an account of the invasion of Judea by Sennacherib, king of Assyria. This is the Jewish record. "In the fourteenth year of Hezekiah, did Sennacherib, king of Assyria, come up against all the fenced cities of Judah, and took them." (2 Kings 18: 13; 2 Chron. 32: 1; Isa. 36: 1.) Compare this record, thrice recorded, apparently by three different hands, with the Assyrian history of the campaign, as preserved on the walls of Sennacherib's palace, to be read in our day for the confirmation of the Scriptures. "Because Hezekiah, king of Judah, did not submit to my yoke, I took and plundered forty-six of his strong fenced cities, and innumerable smaller towns, but I left him Jerusalem, his capital city."

He does not tell us why he left Jerusalem. For the kings of the East were not accustomed to chronicle events that were regarded as discreditable to themselves. Isaiah, however, has supplied the lack. He *intended* to take Jerusalem. He sent his general, Rabshakeh, to demand its surrender. Hezekiah looked to God in prayer, informed Isaiah of their peril, and soon received this message from God: "Sennacherib shall not come into this city, nor shoot an arrow there, nor come before it with shield, nor cast a bank against it. By the way which he came he shall return, saith the Lord. And the angel of the Lord went out and smote in the camp of the Assyrians an hundred and fourscore and five thousand. So Sennacherib, king of Assyria, departed, and went, and returned, and dwelt at Nineveh." (2 Kings 19: 32—36.)

Here are detailed the *reasons* of his return without the overthrow of Judah's capital. A plague broke out miraculously in his army, God's angel, to turn him away from Zion.

There is a singularly explicit passage in the book of Nahum respecting this disastrous invasion, (1: 12) : "Thus saith Jehovah, Though they are unharmed and therefore many, yet nevertheless כֵן נָגֹזּוּ, *they* shall be cut off, וְעָבָר, and *he* shall pass away;" where the prosperity of the invasion up to this hour, the overthrow of the army, and the flight of Sennacherib are all crowded into one verse, the *number* of the verbs being changed to discriminate between the fate of the army, and of their leader.

While Rabshakeh was demanding the surrender of Jerusalem, Sennacherib, his master, was besieging Lachish. "He himself (Sennacherib) laid siege against Lachish, and all his power with him." (2 Chron. 32: 9.) This language implies that the attack of Lachish was a notable event of the campaign. Perhaps one of the most notable. Did the king make any record of it after his return? Yes, and Layard has recently brought it to the light. (See "*Babylon and Nineveh, Second Expedition*," pp. 149—153.) The wall upon which the scene is sculptured is thirty-eight feet in length by eighteen in height. A strongly fortified city is besieged by an army. The banks or mounds of earth are thrown up to aid and protect the besiegers. Seven battering-rams stand before the walls. From the battlements and towers the besieged are seen hurling javelins, stones, and blazing torches upon the assailants, while archers and slingers on either side are contending fiercely for the mastery. Scaling-ladders are brought into requisition. The flames are bursting out here and there, which some are striving to extinguish, others to increase. A part of the city is taken. Prisoners are captured. A procession of these are on their way to the king, who is seated upon a royal throne in sight of the combat. Some of them are being put to the torture. Some lie stretched on the ground to be flayed alive, while others are slain with the sword before the king. To remove all doubt respecting the import of these sculptures, there is an inscription over the head of the king,. recording his order: "Sennacherib, the mighty king, king of the country of Assyria, sitting on the throne of judgment before the city of Lachish, I give permission for its slaughter."

How many incidental circumstances relative to Sennacherib's invasion, and the siege of Lachish are contained on that wall of the conqueror's palace! Every line of those bas-reliefs *is a witness to the veracity of three of the sacred historians.*

In these historical annals of the exploits of Sennacherib, there are indications of the death of the king while the sculptures were in progress. At least, the work was left imperfect. The sculptors stopped before they had completed several of the scenes which they had sketched in outline.

Who could look on those imperfect sculptures, and not be reminded of the last scenes of Sennacherib's life, and of his tragic death, as recorded in the second book of Kings. (19: 36, 37.) "So Sennacherib departed from Judea, and went, and returned, and dwelt at Nineveh. And it came to pass, as he was worshiping in the house of Nisroch, his god, that Adrammelech and Sharezer, his sons, smote him with the sword; and they escaped into the land of Armenia. And Esar-haddon, his son, reigned in his stead."

That he lived some time after his return to Nineveh is evident from the progress of those sculptures, recording his exploits. That he died before all the events of the expedition were intrusted to the sculptors is evident from their unfinished state. It is demonstrable from Assyrian records that the Armenians and Assyrians were at this time hostile to each other, and therefore in a state to invite fugitives from justice in one, to take refuge in the territory of the other, according to the Jewish record. And there is besides an Armenian tradition that speaks distinctly of the murderers, as fleeing to that land, and settling there.

CHAPTER X.

Prophecy of Jonah.—Jonah's Gourd.

THE ruins of Nineveh afford interesting confirmations of the statements of Jonah also, who was sent to prophesy against it. The city is there represented as "an exceeding great city, of three days' journey, (i. e., in circuit,) wherein are more than sixty thousand persons that cannot discern between their right hand and their left hand," (i. e., infants.) (Jon. 4: 11.) Dr. Lobdell has shown, that "Koyunjik, Nimrood, Karamless, and Khorsabad, (all of which are extensive ruins,) mark the corners of a parallelogram, or trapezium, some sixty miles in circuit, all of which was probably once covered with the streets and bazaars, the public and private edifices, and the palaces and parks of Nineveh. The coincidence in dimensions is striking, 'three days' journey' in the East being just sixty miles." (*Memoir of Lobdell.*)

From the same source we have two other illustrations of allusions in the book of Jonah. "On the east side of the city, Jonah made him a booth, and sat under it, in the shadow. And the Lord prepared a gourd, and made it come up over Jonah, that it might be a shadow over his head." (Jon. 4: 5, 6.)

Dr. Lobdell found growing there at the present day "a species of pumpkin-squash, having very large leaves, and trained to run over structures of mud and brush, so as to form booths in which the gardeners protect themselves from the terrible beams of the Asiatic sun." This, by the unanimous verdict of Moslems, Jews, and Christians, at Mosul, is pronounced to be the קִיקָיוֹן of the Hebrew, the gourd of Jonah."

"When the sun did arise, God prepared a vehement east wind, and the sun beat upon the head of Jonah, that he fainted, and wished in himself to die." (Jon. 4: 8.)

Our missionary says: "The east wind (E. S. E.) is not to be mistaken. It withers and prostrates all before it. Clouds of dust and stubble are borne before it, and the hot air almost suffocates one."

Such are some of the verifications of the Scriptures that refer to Nineveh, and the physical features of the lands in the valley of the Tigris. While the desolation that reigns every where on the soil trod by many millions in Old Testament times, is a direct fulfilment of the judgments denounced by the prophets Nahum and Zephaniah. By such evidence we know that they were inspired prophets, uttering not their own maledictions, but the will and plans of God.

CHAPTER XI.

Ezekiel's Vision.—Tammuz.

THE prophet Ezekiel records a singular vision which he had by the river Chebar. Jerusalem seemed to stand before him, and one guided him from place to place, and showed him the great wickedness of the Jewish nation. "Then he brought me," records the prophet, " to the door of the gate of the Lord's house, which was towards the north, and behold there sat women weeping for Tammuz." (Ezek. 8: 14.) A singular vision truly! "Women weeping for Tammuz!" The curtain drops! a new vision is presented, and we hear no more of Tammuz in the Scriptures. What can the vision mean?

The classical scholar is familiar with the fable of Adonis, the son of a Cyprian king, who, fond of the chase, was killed by a wild boar that he had wounded among the mountains of Lebanon. "The river that flowed down the mountain's side was called by his name, and every year, on the anniversary of his death, was said to run blood. And the beautiful red anemone, that abounds in Syria, was supposed to spring up from the earth as a perpetual souvenir." Venus was inconsolable, and obtained from Proserpina the permission, that he should spend six months of the year with her on the earth, and the remaining six in the shades.

Thus much for the fable. But in those

days legends had power to mould the popular belief, and control the rites of religion. They embodied, in fact, the religious opinions of those heathen peoples. And there arose a temple upon the banks of that mountain torrent, and the Grecian and Syrian women annually mourned the death of Adonis, and celebrated its anniversary with idolatrous rites.

Such was the state of things in Syria in the days of Ezekiel. Tammuz was the Syrian name for the Grecian Adonis, whose apotheosis even the Hebrew women had learned to celebrate. Hence the prophet sees this vision "at the gate of the Lord's house which was towards the north," for the temple of Adonis was almost precisely north of Jerusalem, distant about 150 miles.

The river Adonis of the classic authors is

the modern Ibrahim, or Abraham's river. Leaving Beirut, and following the coast northward less than a day's journey, the traveler comes upon this stream, rushing impetuously down a deep and dismal gorge, becoming increasingly furious in the rainy season. Some three hours' travel up this gloomy ravine, and among the overhanging cliffs, and almost impassible precipices, he discovers the ruins of a vast temple. The foundations remain, but the walls are fallen inward, and lie in the utmost disorder. Such was the site of the temple of Venus and Adonis—the Syrian Tammuz. And into those dark defiles multitudes annually crowded to celebrate the death of the Cyprian hunter, and the inconsolable grief of Venus, in rites too licentious to be mentioned. That temple remained until the days of the first Christian emperor. Constantine put an end to its execrable rites by ordering its demolition. But every stone remaining there bears testimony to the idolatry of the Jewish women, and the inspiration of the exiled prophet, Ezekiel.

CHAPTER XII.

Cavern of Bezetha.—Solomon's Temple.

For years to come every visitor to the holy city will account the vast cavern under Bezetha as one of the *lions* of Jerusalem. For centuries it was hid from the knowledge of the world. It was discovered a few years since by Dr. Barclay, Missionary to Jerusalem.

The entrance to this cave is near the Damascus gate, on the north side of the city. It extends under the city, and is about eighty rods in length, and half that distance in breadth. It is an artificial cavern, cut in the solid rock. When, and for what purpose?

Jerusalem visitors have long looked with surprise upon the huge stones at the base of the ancient wall, some of them between twenty and thirty feet in length. There are also immense vaults under the southern part of the temple area, constructed of Roman arches, which are sustained by numerous rows of square pillars, four feet in diameter, some of which are thirty-five feet in height. They are of the same material as the immense blocks in the temple wall, and belong to the same style of architecture. They carry us back to the time when the foundations of the temple were laid, of course to the age of Solomon and his master builders.

The question has often been asked, "Where were those huge blocks quarried, and how were they transported to the summit of Moriah?" The discovery which enables us to answer these questions, affords several interesting verifications of the Jewish record. Let us recall the account of Solomon's labors. "The king commanded and they brought great stones, costly stones, hewed stones, to lay the foundations of the house. And Solomon's builders did hew, and the stone-squarers; so they prepared timber and stones to build the house. And the house was built of stone made ready before it was brought thither; so that there was neither hammer, nor axe, nor any tool of iron heard in the house while it was in building." (1 Kings 5: 17, 18; 6: 7.)

Read now this history standing by the Damascus gate, near the mouth of that vast quarry, and how credible and luminous does every word become. Enter that cavern, and behold the blocks of stone half quarried, still adhering to the rock, showing the process by which they were detached, and the kinds of tools used in elaborating them; for "their marks are as plain, and well defined, as if the workman had but just ceased from his labors." (*City of the Great King*, p. 446.)

The floor of the quarry is covered with the chips and *debris*, caused by the elaborate finish of the columns and arches there, that "neither hammer, nor axe, nor any tool of iron might be heard in the house while it was in building." How easily too were those blocks, when quarried, transported to their present positions! For Bezetha overlooks the temple area, the mouth of the cave beneath it being several feet higher than the foundations of the house. Quarried, and trimmed, and beveled, those massive blocks might easily have been conveyed to their present positions on rollers. And this supposition is at once suggested, we may almost say *proved*, by an allusion in a letter of the enemies of the Jews to Darius, as recorded by Ezra. They say, "The house of the great God is builded with *great stones*," literally, "*stones of rolling*," i. e., so large as to be transported on rollers, and hence, "great stones."

CHAPTER XIII.

Early Spread of Christianity.—Persecutions.— Catacombs of Rome.—Sculptures.

THE New Testament as well as the Old, furnishes abundant incidental evidence that its several parts are inspired. We will select a few illustrations only from the many that might be adduced.

There are several statements of Luke and Paul that imply a wonderfully rapid spread of Christianity, in the latter part of the first, and the beginning of the second centuries. "The Word of God increased, and the number of disciples increased in Jerusalem greatly, and a great number of the priests were obedient to the faith." (Acts 6 : 7.) In narrating the death of Herod Agrippa, which took place some ten years after the ascension of Christ, it is said again,—" The Word of God grew and multiplied." (Acts 12 : 24.) Nor was this rapid spread of the truth confined to Palestine. A few years later than the event just referred to, Paul is preaching at Ephesus. He confounds the Jewish exorcists, the Holy Spirit falls on Jews and Greeks alike, and the testimony is again repeated,—" So mightily grew the Word of God and multiplied." (Acts 19 : 20.) Follow Paul to Rome. He assembles the Jews at once, and begins to preach Christ to them. Some believed as soon as they heard the truth. And converting " his own hired house " into a chapel, he preaches at least two years, and gathers a church at the capital of the Roman Empire.

His Epistles written during that imprisonment indicate the progress of the truth. "My bonds in Christ are manifest in all the palace, and in all other places. And many of the brethren in the Lord, waxing confident by my bonds, are much more bold to speak the Word without fear." (Phil. 1: 13, 14.) In the closing salutation of this epistle, he adds, "The brethren that are with me greet you. All the saints salute you, chiefly they that are of Cæsar's household." (4: 21, 22.)

Here are indications that even in Paul's day the gospel had taken deep root at Rome. What scenes of persecution must have transpired then at the very capital of the world, during those centuries when Pagan emperors "set themselves against the Lord, and against his anointed!"

There has recently come to light monumental evidence respecting the spread of truth, and the persecutions that followed, no less interesting than that which we have gleaned from the exhumed palaces of Nineveh and Babylon. It is but a few years since the Catacombs, those wondrous vaults under the "eternal city," filled with the bones of the martyrs and early Christians, were explored, and these relics brought to the light. What scenes of distress and of triumph were enacted in those eight or nine hundred miles of streets, no imagination can picture. It has been computed that no less than six or seven millions of souls found a retreat and a grave there, though only a few feet of earth separated them from their foes. What a commentary are these vast sand-pits, filled with the bones of ten generations of Christians, upon some of the words of the apostle who preached the gospel there!

"They wandered about in sheep-skins, and goat-skins, being destitute, afflicted, tormented, (of whom the world was not worthy,) they wandered in deserts, and in mountains, and in *dens and caves of the earth.*" (Heb. 11: 37, 38.)

And there they slept. And how beautiful the coincidence between the words of the apostle, "I would not have you ignorant, brethren, concerning them that are asleep,— them also which sleep in Jesus," (1 Thess. 4: 13—15;) and the rude epitaphs carved upon those Christians' tombs! Every where the words, "*In pace*" (in peace) meet the eye. Every inscription attests the *Christian faith* of the sleeper; many a one the *martyrdom.*

"In Christ. In the time of the Emperor Adrian, Marius, a young military officer, who had lived long enough, when with blood he gave up his life for Christ. He rests in peace."

"In Christ. Alexander is not dead, but lives among the stars. While on his knees, and about to sacrifice to the true God, he was led away to execution."

These simple testimonies to the faith and martyrdom of the dead, often carved in the mortar with the trowel of the mason, are an eloquent testimony to the manly, sinewy piety of the early martyrs. "They counted all things but loss, that they might win Christ." (Phil. 3: 8.) What a meaning do the scenes through which they are here seen to have passed, give to those other words of the apostle in bonds, "If in this life only we have hope in Christ, we are of all men most miserable." (1 Cor. 15: 19.) Every grave in those dark recesses is radiant with the hope of immortality.

In the rude specimens of art that are found there, they expressed their faith in the great facts of Old Testament history, as we now receive them. There are pictured the temptation in the garden; the sacrifice of Isaac; Moses striking the rock; Elijah ascending to heaven; Daniel in the lions' den; his three companions in the fiery furnace; and Jonah devoured by a whale, and vomited on dry land. These scripture facts were evidently received as *literal truths*, not as myths and fables. And yet they had been taught the Scriptures by the immediate descendants of the apostles.

There too are sketched the visit of the Magi to the infant Saviour; the baptism of Christ; the healing of the paralytic; the turning of water into wine; the feeding of five thousand; the raising of Lazarus; the last supper; and the crucifixion. Thus have we their testimony to the interpretation of the New Testament facts. It was in the faith of these, as literal truths of history, and of the doctrines that underlie them, that they suffered the loss of all things, and hid themselves in the caves beneath the proud pagan city.

As we look on those sacred mementoes of their suffering lives, we feel that we are one in the faith of Christ, and the interpretation of the Scriptures. We turn away repeating with a quickened faith that precious clause of the apostle's creed, "I believe in the communion of saints."

CHAPTER XIV.

Paul at Athens.—At Ephesus.—The Goddess Diana.—Asiarchs.—Town Clerk.

As an example of the accuracy and trustworthiness of the New Testament writers, let us consult the narrative of Paul's visit to Athens. "His spirit," it is said, "was stirred within him when he saw the city wholly given to idolatry." (Acts 17: 16.) But Athens is the city of which Xenophon testified, "πόλις ὅλη βωμὸς, ὅλη θῦμα θεοῖς καὶ ἀνάθημα." "*The whole city is an altar, the whole a sacrifice to the gods, and a votive offering.*" Of which Livy wrote, "*Athenæ simulacra deorum hominumque habentes, omnigenere et materiæ et artium insignia.*" "Athens, having statues of gods and men of every variety both of material and style of art." Josephus too, in his reply to Apion, shows that the *religiousness* of the Athenians was proverbial. "Apion, who hath no regard to the misfortunes of the Athenians, or of the Lacedemonians, the latter of whom were styled by all men the most courageous, and the former *the most religious of the Grecians.*"

How true to the character of the Athenians is that parenthetic clause thrown casually in, revealing an accurate knowledge of Athenian society. "We would know," said the philosophers, "what these things mean. (For all the Athenians and strangers which were there, spent their time in nothing else, but either to tell or hear some new thing.)" Athens was the city to which strangers would naturally resort for sight-seeing. And the greediness of the Athenians for novelty is well illustrated by a question of Demosthenes, "Tell me, Do you wish to go about in the market place asking each other, What is the news?"

Paul has been preaching upwards of two years at Ephesus. At length a tumult is excited by Demetrius and his fellow-craftsmen. The rabble gathers at the theatre. The silversmiths make an harangue, showing the dangers that threaten the worship of Diana. "And all with one voice about the space of two hours cried out, Great is Diana of the Ephesians." (Acts 19: 34.) Until recently it was not known that the title *Great Goddess* had been specially given to Diana among the Greeks. But about a century ago a manuscript of Xenophon was discovered, in a passage of which a virgin is represented as swearing by the goddess of her native city. "'Ομνύω την πατριον ημιν Θεόν την μεγάλην Εφεσίων "Αρτεμιν." "*I invoke our ancestral god, the great Diana of the Ephesians.*" An inscription too has been brought to light containing the same phrase, " της μεγάλης Θεάς "Ερτεμιδος."

"And certain of *the chief* of Asia," (τινὲς τῶν 'Ασιαρχων) protected Paul. (Acts 19: 31.) These Ephesian *Asiarchs* also are referred to on coins and inscriptions. "They were ten in number, selected by the cities to preside over the public worship, and approved by the proconsul; of whom one was the chief, and always resided at Ephesus, the capital; the others were his colleagues and advisers." (Rob. Gr. Lex.)

As the tumult increases, the "town clerk" (ὁ γραμματεὺς) comes forward and "appeases the people." (19: 35.) There have been found three inscriptions in which this officer is mentioned. The speech of the town clerk, by which he appeased the people, furnishes another incidental allusion that proves the genuineness of the narrative. "Ye men of Ephesus, what man is there that knoweth not how that the city of the Ephesians is *a worshiper* (νεωκόρον) of the great goddess Diana." (Acts 19: 35.) The title *Neoeoros*, literally *temple-sweeper*, applied at first to the lowest menials who had the care of the temple, became an *honorable* title, and was appropriated by the city, and stamped upon its coins. These therefore afford the means of illustrating the allusion, and proving the accuracy of the historian.

CHAPTER XV.

Roman Government as seen in "Luke" and "The Acts of the Apostles."

How accurately is the Roman Government depicted in the Acts, wherever there are incidental allusions to it! Cæsar, the Emperor, is on the throne. "I stand at Cæsar's judgment seat, where I ought to be judged. I appeal unto Cæsar." (Acts 25: 10, 11.) And to Cæsar is he sent. The Provinces, however, were governed by *proconsuls*. And Luke alludes to the proconsuls of Cyprus, Ephesus, and Achaia by the classic Greek term 'Ανδυπάιος. Now the moment a historian descends to particulars, we are able to test the accuracy of his narrative. And we ask, Was Cyprus at that time under proconsular authority? Formerly it was a *pretorian* province. But both Strabo and Dio Cassius assert, that Augustus, the ancestor of the then reigning Cæsar, had "given it up to the people, and so *proconsuls* began to be sent." This title is found on Cyprian coins, and in an inscription of the reign of Claudius, the predecessor of Nero. Luke then was exact. Cyprus was *at that time* governed by proconsuls, though a short time previous it was *not* so governed.

"Gallio was proconsul of Achaia," says Luke, at the time Paul was preaching at Corinth, its capital city. (Acts 18: 12.) Are we able to verify *this* historic allusion? According to the testimony of Dio Cassius, Achaia was *originally* a senatorial province, and of course governed by proconsuls. But

Tacitus relates that Tiberius took it into his own keeping, and governed it by *legates* during his reign. From the life of Claudius, by Suetonius, we learn that in the fourth year of his reign this monarch restored it to the senate, from which time it was governed by proconsuls again. But the fourth year of the reign of Claudius was only two years before Paul's visit to Corinth.

How easily an uninformed, unreliable historian might have mistaken here. But we find no tripping in our author. He is minutely accurate in the whole narrative. In his Providence, God has preserved the evidence of this accuracy in the profane annals of that age.

CHAPTER XVI.

" The Foolish Galatians."—The French.

PAUL had preached the gospel to the Galatians with great acceptance. Alluding to their enthusiasm, and the ardor of their attachment, he says in his letter to them, (Gal. 4: 15,) " I bear you record, that if it had been possible ye would have plucked out your own eyes, and have given them to me." After his departure, however, Judaizing teachers came in, and turned their minds against him. Hence the strong chidings of his epistle. "I marvel that ye are so soon removed from him that called you unto the grace of Christ, unto another gospel."

(Gal. 1: 6.) "O, foolish Galatians, who hath bewitched you, that ye should not obey the truth? Are ye so foolish? Having begun in the spirit, are ye now made perfect by the flesh?" (Gal. 3: 1, 3.)

These reproofs indicate an exceedingly fickle nation, fond of novelty, enthusiastic in the extreme, but—

"To nothing fixed but *love of change.*"

Were these the characteristics of the Galatians? Callimachus calls them a "foolish people." Hilary, who was himself a Gaul, and Jerome, both use the phrase "*Gallos indociles,*" unteachable, or intractable Gauls; fully justifying Paul's language as referring to an *acknowledged national characteristic.*

There is another source of presumptive evidence. Who were those Galatians?

Originally inhabited by the Greeks, the province of Galatia was conquered by the Gauls from western Europe, about two centuries and a half before the Christian era. Strabo calls it Γαλλο-γραικία, (Gallo-Graecia, hence by contraction, Galatia,) from this intermingling of the Gallic and Hellenistic races. We may expect, therefore, to find at Galatia the national characteristics of the Gauls. These characteristics are still seen in the French nation, who inhabit the country then known as Gaul, and who have descended from the same ancestors as the conquerors of the Asiatic Galatia.

How striking a confirmation of the words of Paul, "Foolish Galatians—so soon removed from him that called you—bewitched—beginning in the spirit, to be made perfect in the flesh," is afforded by the recent history of the French nation! In a little more than half a century, they have passed through as many revolutions as there are days in a week. And yet they have always been enthusiastic, and full of admiration for the last governmental novelty, easily adjusting themselves to types and characteristics of government the most directly opposite to each other. "Vive l' Assemblée!" "Vive la Republique!" "Vive l' Empereur!" "Vive le Roi!" "Vive le Président!" and "Vive l' Empereur!" have been vociferated in rapid succession; and through all these changes, the people have been buoyant, but never provident; loving liberty, and yet fitfully submitting to tyranny and oppression; rising in spasms to be free, but never cool, never calculating, never fixed in their purpose, never religious in their aim, never prayerful; and so God forsakes them, and turns their counsels into foolishness, and makes them a standing verification of the truthfulness of Paul's delineation of their character—"Foolish, bewitched Galatians!"

Turn which way we will we find something to illustrate and confirm the veracity of the Scriptures, and the inspiration of the men who wrote them. Scan their representations as closely as we may, we cannot convict them of error, I will not say, in the great outlines and leading themes of which they treat only, but even in the thousand casual allusions to places, persons, characters, governments, officers, laws, revolutions, the founding or overthrow of cities and nations. No where else within the range of literature can such exactness and precision be found. It is more than human; it proves itself Divine.

GLEANINGS FROM SCIENCE, ART, ETC. 95

CHAPTER XVII.

Science.—Circulation of the Blood.—Weight of the Atmosphere.—The Pleiades.—The Firmament.

IN scientific circles there has been a ceaseless effort to invalidate the statements of Inspiration. In the infancy of almost every science, scepticism has *seemed* to see principles and data opposed to the Bible. The Scriptures cannot be called *scientific* writings, it is true; that is, they were not designed to teach the sciences of any age. Nevertheless, it is found as science advances, that its laws have been anticipated and presupposed in the Hebrew Scriptures.

According to the statements of Moses, it would seem that previously to the flood, flesh was not eaten as food. After that event, God said to Noah, "Every moving thing that liveth shall be meat for you. But flesh with the life thereof, (which is the blood thereof,) shall ye not eat." (Gen. 9: 3, 4.) In the formal announcement of the Levitical Law, it is three times repeated. "The life of the flesh is in the blood." (Lev. 17: 11, 14; Deut. 12: 23.) Here was announced a great physiological truth. And on it was based a law, which the Jewish nation were to observe through all their generations, forbidding them to eat blood. This law was very imperative, and was designed to make the blood sacred in their esteem; "Because it is the blood that maketh an atonement for the soul." (Lev. 17: 11.) God was disciplining the world for the reception of his Son, and the exercise of faith in his blood. Hence the so earnest announcement and reiteration of this truth —*Blood, the life of the flesh.* And yet with the help of Moses' statement of this law, from the lips of God, men of science have not believed it until recently. It was reserved for Harvey and Hunter of the last century to discover the office of the blood, and to enunciate the truth which God revealed to Moses, more than 3,000 years ago.

A recent Essay in Blackwood's Magazine, upon the " Wonders and Curiosities of the Blood," opens with this paragraph: " Blood is the mighty river of life, the mysterious centre of chemical and vital actions." An important scientific truth, established by a long series of experiments. But Moses affirmed it thirty centuries since. How did he alone of all the race know it? He was not accustomed to dissect human bodies. He was neither a Physiologist nor a Physician. No other answer can be given, that is at all satisfactory, except this,—It was directly revealed to him, as he affirms, by Him who knows all the secrets of the animal economy. He was employed to make known a truth, which it took the world a score and a half of centuries to discover.

Age after age men have read the beautiful aphorisms of the book of Job. But who has understood, until these later days, the deep meaning of the statement, "He maketh the weight for the winds," or as Barnes has more literally translated it, "To the winds he gave weight." (Job 28: 25.) Only about 230 years have passed since Galileo was imprisoned by the Holy Inquisition for interpreting the Scriptures in accordance with the revelations of his telescope. It was during that imprisonment that he was applied to by an artisan to solve this question in hydrostatics: *" Why will water rise in a vacuum only* 32 *feet?"* Galileo believed it was the " weight of the winds," i. e., of the atmosphere, that caused the water to rise. But the fear of the Inquisition hushed the thought, and he gave the evasive reply: *" Nature abhors a vacuum only to the height of* 32 *feet."*

The truth, that was then suppressed, has since his day been demonstrated, and received. The *exact weight* of the winds is known. The truth which Job asserted in the oldest book in existence is at length believed. God taught it to the world by the man of Uz, more than 3,000 years ago. But men of science have not been willing to receive their data from this source, and hence for centuries they have remained in ignorance of this scientific truth.

"Canst thou bind the sweet influences of the Pleiades?" said God to Job, in that series of interrogatories that overwhelmed him with self-abhorrence and penitence. Is there not here a beautiful poetic allusion to the apparent attraction of the Pleiades for the sun and planets? Astronomers tell us that our solar system is moving towards the star Alcyon, one of this group, as though drawn by its "sweet influences." Who but He who "holds the stars in his right hand, and spreads out the heavens like a curtain," could have known that fact, in that patriarchal age? It has taken centuries of observation and experiment, with the aid of the most accurate instruments, to determine it. Job recorded, most manifestly, what was revealed to him from the Author of all the laws of the universe.

Until recently, the rotundity of the earth has been accounted heresy in all scientific circles. But Isaiah exclaimed concerning God, "It is He that sitteth upon *the circle* of the earth," חוּג הָאָרֶץ, "*Orbis terrarum,*" Rob. Lex.

In Moses' account of the creation of the world, he says, (Gen. 1: 6.) "And God said, Let there be *a firmament* in the midst of the waters, and let it divide the waters from the waters." The word rendered "*firmament*" is רָקִיעַ, an expanse, something *spread out, extended,* i. e., space without sensible limit. But when the Old Testament was translated into Greek, (B. C. 250,) the word στερέωμα, any thing *hard, firm, solid,* was adopted as its synonym; for such was the opinion of that age concerning it. The Vulgate, (A. D. 383,) following the erroneous example, rendered the word by "*firmamentum;*" and our English version, (A. D. 1611,) by "*firmament.*" It appears then that Moses was *scientifically exact* in his expression of the historic fact, according to the *modern theory of the heavens*, a theory based on evidence that cannot be shaken. How was he able, in the days of the Pharaohs, to write with greater scientific and philologic exactness, than the most learned Jews, of the days of Ptolemy, the critical, "the scientific period" of Grecian literature? The question admits of but one answer. Moses was *inspired of God* to write that which should be consistent with all the facts of nature; which should therefore anticipate the discoveries and principles of science, and be seen to correspond with them. His translators were not so inspired. They carried therefore the errors of the ages in which they lived into their translations.

The believer in the inspiration of the Scriptures has no cause, then, to fear the disclosures of science. As yet, *no one* fact has been produced, or law discovered, which is in conflict with Revelation. Every feature of science, *when fully wrought out, and its bearings seen*, confirms and illustrates what "holy men of old wrote, when they were moved by the Holy Ghost."

CHAPTER XVIII.

Manners and Customs of Bible Lands.

THE allusions of travelers to the habits and customs of Bible lands afford interesting circumstantial evidence of the inspiration of the Scriptures. The dress of the inhabitants; the methods of irrigating and tilling the soil; of threshing and winnowing the grain; of burying the dead, and beautifying their sepulchres, all correspond with the scenery of the Bible. Every page of Scripture is said to be *luminous*, when read amidst the stereotype customs of Egypt, Palestine or Assyria. There are the "women grinding at the mill," as in the days of Christ. There the shepherds "going out before their flocks, calling them all by name, and known by every sheep." There are the numerous yokes of oxen attached to the same plough, as when Elishah ploughed with twelve, as Elijah met him, and threw his mantle over him. There too is the concourse of citizens at the gate of the city, for traffic, marriage, controversy, and judgment; as when Lot was found by the angels sitting in the gate of Sodom; as when Boaz took to him the Moabitess, Ruth, and redeemed her possession; as when David complained that those that "sat in the gate reviled him;" and Solomon extolled the husband of the virtuous woman as one "known in the gates, and sitting among the elders of the land;" or as when Matthew was called from the "seat of custom," in this place of concourse. And there also are seen the "cottage in the vineyard, and the lodge in the garden of cucumbers," and in the desert is heard the braying of the wild ass, and the passing traveler sees him "snuff up the wind," and gallop away in the distance, as he was accustomed to do in the days of the sufferer of Uz.

And thus every page of the Scriptures is authenticated, by all we know of the manners, customs and rites of the orientals. They furnish the fullest proof possible, that they were written at the age they purport to have been written, and amidst the scenes and customs from which their illustrations are drawn.

CHAPTER XIX.

Conclusion.

THIS incidental, indirect testimony might be increased almost at pleasure. It is continually accumulating, never before so rapidly as at this age, when the antiquarian, the traveler, and the missionary are exhuming the relics of all those sacred lands, where the scenes of Scripture history were laid.

This evidence, by itself alone, when collected together, would be sufficient to establish the Divine origin of the Scriptures. It could be accounted for upon no other assumption.

We need not then resort to *presumptive*

evidence, and say, *God would naturally make known his will to men*; we need not show that all parts of the Scriptures are so interlinked by *prophecies and their fulfilment* after the lapse of centuries, as to bar all doubt in the candid mind; we need not turn to the *miraculous powers* of those whom God employed to write the Scriptures, as proof that they were divinely commissioned; or to *the contents* of the sacred writings themselves, revealing as they do a purer morality, and holier precepts than man uninspired has ever originated in any age or nation; or to *their effects* upon the hearts and lives of men, as they have gone out to develop humanity, to civilize and Christianize the race. We may turn away from these more *direct* proofs that "all Scripture is given by Inspiration of God,"— but we shall find all science, all history, all antiquarian relics, all ethnographic discoveries, all the memoranda of travelers, and all passing events uttering the same testimony. The starry constellations will repeat it. The deep strata of the earth, the currents of the ocean, and the aerial tides that distribute the waters that are above the firmament will echo the momentous, the joyful truth,—THE SCRIPTURES ARE THE WORD OF GOD, THE INFALLIBLE RULE OF DUTY. Yes, and every Infidel, as Hume and Gibbon, and the madder host of rationalists of our day have done, will help to confirm it.

THE END.

www.ingramcontent.com/pod-product-compliance
Lightning Source LLC
Chambersburg PA
CBHW021944160426
43195CB00011B/1220